Explore
the Bible ®

Let the Word dwell in you.

MW01007116

Dewey Decimal Classification Number: 227.87

Subject Heading: BIBLE. N.T. HEBREWS-STUDY\ CHRISTIAN LIFE

ERIC GEIGER
Vice President, Church Resources

DAVID JEREMIAH
General Editor

TOBY JENNINGS
Managing Editor

JEREMY MAXFIELD
Content Editor

FAITH WHATLEY
Director, Adult Ministry

PHILIP NATION
Director, Adult Ministry Publishing

With Explore the Bible, groups can expect to engage Scripture in its proper context and be better prepared to live it out in their own context. These book-by-book studies will help participants...

> grow in their love for Scripture.

> gain new knowledge about what the Bible teaches.

> develop biblical disciplines.

> internalize the Word in a way that transforms their lives.

Send questions/comments to: Content Editor, *Explore the Bible: Adult Small Group Study*, One LifeWay Plaza, Nashville, TN 37234-0152

Printed in the United States of America

For ordering or inquiries visit *www.lifeway.com*, or write LifeWay Small Groups, One LifeWay Plaza, Nashville, TN 37234-0152; or call toll free 800.458.2772.

 Connect

@ExploreTheBible

facebook.com/ExploreTheBible

lifeway.com/ExploreTheBible

ministrygrid.com/web/ExploreTheBible

1

❯ ABOUT THIS STUDY

CHRISTIANS CAN LOSE THEIR CONFIDENCE IN THE LORD. MAYBE YOU'RE ONE OF THEM.

Perhaps you're at a point when you're wondering if you can keep on trusting Him. Life has been tough, and hard times seem to be getting harder. Your circumstances are making you wonder if you need to step back from Jesus for a while.

The Book of Hebrews can give you the spiritual refreshment you need. It's a book that helps struggling Christians get a fresh perspective on Jesus, resulting in a fresh burst of courage to endure in faith.

Explore the Bible: Hebrews, Chapters 1-7 helps you know and apply the encouraging and empowering truth of God's Word by organizing each session in the following way:

UNDERSTAND THE CONTEXT: This page explains the original context of each passage and begins relating the primary themes to your life today.

EXPLORE THE TEXT: This section walks you through the Scripture, providing helpful commentary and encouraging thoughtful interaction with God through His Word.

OBEY THE TEXT: This section helps you apply the truths you have explored. It is not enough to know what the Bible says—God's Word has the power to change your life.

LEADER GUIDE: This final section provides optional discussion starters and suggested questions to help anyone lead a group in reviewing each section of the personal study.

❯GROUP COMMITMENT

As you begin this study, it is important that everyone agree to key group values. Clearly establishing the purpose of your time together will foster healthy expectations and help ease any uncertainties. The goal is to ensure that everyone has a positive experience leading to spiritual growth and true community. Initial each value as you discuss the following with your group.

❏ PRIORITY

Life is busy but we value this time with one another and with God's Word. We choose to make being together a priority.

❏ PARTICIPATION

We are a group. Everyone is encouraged to participate. No one dominates.

❏ RESPECT

Everyone is given the right to his or her own opinions. All questions are encouraged and respected.

❏ TRUST

Each person will humbly seek truth through time in prayer and in the Bible. We will trust God as the loving authority in our lives.

❏ CONFIDENTIALITY

Anything said in our meetings will never be repeated outside of the group without permission from everyone involved. This is vital in creating an environment of trust and openness.

❏ SUPPORT

Everyone can count on anyone in this group. Permission is given to call upon each other at any time, especially in times of crisis. The group will provide care for every member.

❏ ACCOUNTABILITY

We agree to let the members of our group hold us accountable to commitments we make in the loving ways we decide upon. Questions are always welcome. Unsolicited advice, however, is not permitted.

_____   _____

I agree to all of the above   date

❯ GENERAL EDITOR

 **Dr. David Jeremiah** serves as senior pastor of Shadow Mountain Community Church in El Cajon, California. He is the founder and host of Turning Point, committed to providing Christians with sound Bible teaching relevant to today's changing times through radio and television, the Internet, live events, and resource materials and books. A best-selling author, Dr. Jeremiah has written more than 40 books, including *What Are You Afraid Of?* and its companion small group study, and his study notes from over four decades have been compiled into *The Jeremiah Study Bible*.

Dr. Jeremiah's commitment to teaching the complete Word of God continues to make him a sought-after speaker and writer. His passion for reaching the lost and encouraging believers in their faith is demonstrated through his faithful communication of biblical truths.

A dedicated family man, Dr. Jeremiah and his wife, Donna, have 4 grown children and 11 grandchildren.

❯ CONTENTS

WHO IS JESUS?

As God's Son, Jesus revealed God finally and without equal.

❯ UNDERSTAND THE CONTEXT

PREPARE FOR YOUR GROUP EXPERIENCE WITH THE FOLLOWING PAGES.

There's a lot of talk about Jesus these days. But does anyone really know who they're talking about? The name of Jesus can be found everywhere from t-shirts and bumper stickers to celebrity speeches. It can be confusing, at best, to sort through all of the noise. So who is Jesus, really? And why does it matter? These same questions have been asked for 2000 years.

The writer of Hebrews set out to help troubled Christians see Jesus as the Son of God, the only way to eternal life and earthly fulfillment. Jesus wasn't merely one of the many voices through whom God spoke to His creation. He spoke as God's Son. That relationship makes Him superior to the prophets and the angels. He alone was the full revelation of God to all people everywhere.

His nature, His involvement in creating and nurturing the universe, His death on the cross for our purification, and His exaltation demonstrate that God the Father and God the Son are equally God. Shaped by such a powerful perspective, we can share with confidence God's life-changing message of redemption.

In the Book of Hebrews, Jesus is the centerpiece of Christianity—the Son of God, our High Priest, the Source and Perfecter of our faith—and the list could go on. The writer addressed a variety of questions reinforcing Christ's superiority in the lives of His followers. As you explore the Book of Hebrews, make careful note of who Jesus is and hold tightly to your faith in the exalted Christ.

CHALLENGE

Be aware of the various opinions about Jesus in today's culture. Search the Book of Hebrews and the rest of God's Word for the truth.

"NEVER HAS THE BIBLICAL JESUS BEEN DRAGGED THROUGH THE MUD LIKE HE IS IN THIS CURRENT CULTURE."

—*David Jeremiah*

▶ HEBREWS 1:1-4

1 Long ago God spoke to the fathers by the prophets at different times and in different ways.

2 In these last days, He has spoken to us by His Son. God has appointed Him heir of all things and made the universe through Him.

3 The Son is the radiance of God's glory and the exact expression of His nature, sustaining all things by His powerful word. After making purification for sins, He sat down at the right hand of the Majesty on high.

4 So He became higher in rank than the angels, just as the name He inherited is superior to theirs.

Think About It

After reading Hebrews 1:1-4, circle the various descriptions of Jesus.

In your own words, explain how the descriptions in these verses impact your relationship with Jesus.

⟩ ABOUT THE BOOK OF HEBREWS

AUTHOR

The writer of Hebrews didn't identify himself, and Bible scholars haven't been able to determine who wrote it. Though we don't know the writer's identity, his spiritual maturity is evident within his writing. His writing reflected a devoted Christian leader who displayed passionate concern about believers considering retreat from Christianity.

AUDIENCE

Concerning the Christians to whom the Book of Hebrews was addressed, we can discern from the comparisons drawn in the text to key components of Judaism that they were believers, primarily from a Jewish background, who didn't have a clear understanding of who Jesus was. The persecution they were experiencing had caused them to reconsider their commitment to Christ, even being tempted to return to their traditional Jewish roots. Perhaps some of their friends and family members had been mistreated because of Christ. Or maybe they had experienced hard times themselves at the hands of adversaries of the gospel.

The strain of persecution apparently had been tempting them to consider an escape route. They still wanted to worship God, but they didn't want to live with the risk of more persecution. Details within the text suggest some were leaning toward returning to Judaism as an alternative. In their decision to embrace a safer way to serve God, they began distancing themselves from other Christians. The writer wanted them to work through any disillusionment by staying focused on Jesus and His superiority in their lives. Ultimately, they needed to be reminded of who He is.

PURPOSE

The writer of Hebrews made a passionate effort to persuade Christ-followers to maintain their faith in Jesus. He urged them to affirm the superiority of Christ above everything and everyone they had read about in the Old Testament. Then he encouraged them to consider God's perspective in their decision to possibly walk away from faith in Christ. Seeing themselves through God's eyes, they would surely understand why He would hold them accountable for misguided acts of disobedience and rebellion. Finally, he challenged them to hold fast to the gospel, no matter the circumstances.

❯ EXPLORE THE TEXT

GOD SPEAKS (Read Hebrews 1:1-2a.)

Hebrews begins with a comparison between how God spoke in the "former days"—the Old Testament times—and how He has spoken in the "latter days"—after the incarnation of Christ. The writer isn't pushing the Old Testament to the side as if it's no longer relevant. The Bible is a cohesive whole with God's Son at the center.

The Christ-followers receiving this letter appeared to be struggling with the temptation to return to Old Testament Judaism. If that was the case, it would stand to reason that the writer would point to the Old Testament prophets. He used what was familiar to them as the starting point for his case for Christ.

In His wisdom, God spoke to the forefathers of the Old Testament through the prophets. God raised up prophets at different times to speak for Him. Moses prophesied at a specific time in history. So did Elijah, Elisha, Isaiah, Jeremiah, Malachi, and all the other prophets. John the Baptist took on the prophetic role in the New Testament, preparing the way for the coming Messiah. God called the prophets to proclaim His Word at just the right time for the people who needed to hear and apply it in their situations.

Each of these prophets preached God's Word in different ways. Some of them spoke through thundering sermons and gripping stories. Other prophets used piercing word pictures and remarkable miracles as they delivered God's message. Still others spoke to God's people with careful insights and courageous wisdom. Through a variety of approaches and styles, they delivered God's message.

What do verses 1-2a teach about God's desire and ability to communicate with His people?

The writer went on to make a confident declaration: What God said through the prophets long ago couldn't be considered His final word. On the contrary, God continued to speak. When the writer mentioned "these last days," he had in mind the arrival of Jesus. God spoke through Jesus in a way that rose high above the messages of the prophets. God Himself, in the person of Jesus Christ, was now speaking. There was no middle-man.

GOD REVEALED
(Read Hebrews 1:2b-4.)

The writer of Hebrews went on to explain why Jesus surpassed the prophets as God's complete revelation to the world. He described Jesus as God's heir. God owned all things in the universe. Like a king in a royal court, the God of the universe appointed His own Son to inherit everything He had created, both in heaven and on earth. Jesus was more than an heir. He was involved in the creation of everything. The Father made everything that's eternal as well as everything that's temporary through His Son. With that affirmation, the writer of Hebrews nailed down the eternal truth that Jesus existed before the universe was created.

Along with inheriting everything created, Jesus also radiates God's glory (see Col. 1:15). He alone shines with the splendor of God's presence in the world. However, He doesn't serve as radiance in the way the moon reflects light from the sun. Instead, the Son emanates the glory of the Father because He is God.

**Bible Skill:
Dig deeper using other Scripture to better understand a passage**

Read these passages in your Bible:

• Genesis 1:26

• Colossians 1:15-18

• John 1:1-4

How do these verses deepen your understanding of what Hebrews 1 reveals about Jesus' eternal existence?

The writer of Hebrews shows us something else about Jesus that reinforced His superiority. Copy machines produce duplicates of the original document. Look closely, and you can probably tell the difference between the original document and the copy. That's not the case with Jesus. He's the exact expression of God. In other words, the Son is the original—exactly like the Father. Because He's the original, He exhibits the fullness of God's divine nature. Therefore, He guides and upholds all of creation. He carries out His sustaining work in the universe in a way that shows that He's God. He utters His powerful word to nourish and direct His creation.

Directing us to observe Christ's work in history, the writer points us to the cross. The crucified Christ made complete the purification for our sins. Now the risen Lord has been exalted on high. He has taken His seat at the right hand of the Father in majesty. When He sat down in that exalted place, it was a declaration of His completed work that was necessary for our salvation and demonstrates His equality with the Father. His powerful reign is limitless.

The writer of Hebrews presented troubled Christians with warranted reasons for staying true to Christ as they faced potential persecution. Having already shown Jesus' superiority to the prophets, he directed them to realize that Jesus reigned over the angels, who enjoyed a position of high rank in God's kingdom. Like the prophets, angels also would've been viewed as messengers sent from God. Jesus reigned supreme over them for one undeniable reason: He alone bore God's matchless name. God, the Son, inherited the name of God, the Father. Therefore, He is God.

Have you ever felt persecuted for your faith?

In what ways did that persecution challenge your beliefs?

Key Doctrine: Scripture and Jesus

All Scripture is a testimony to Christ, who is Himself the focus of divine revelation. See Matthew 5:17; Luke 24:27; John 5:39.

❯ OBEY THE TEXT

Jesus is the full revelation of God to humanity. Through Him, we can understand God's character and the gospel message. As God reveals Himself to us, we can share that truth with others.

How has God revealed Himself to you recently?

What actions are you taking as a result?

How can you help your group create an environment that fosters the open sharing of truths God reveals?

MEMORIZE

"In these last days, He has spoken to us by His Son" (Hebrews 1:2a).

Use the space provided to make observations and record prayer requests during the group experience for this session.

MY THOUGHTS

Record insights and questions from the group experience.

_____
_____
_____
_____
_____
_____

MY RESPONSE

Note specific ways you will put into practice the truth explored this week.

_____
_____
_____
_____
_____
_____

MY PRAYERS

List specific prayer needs and answers to remember this week.

_____
_____
_____
_____
_____
_____

A GREAT SALVATION

Believers must diligently guard against drifting away from their confession of Jesus.

❯ UNDERSTAND THE CONTEXT

In life we need warnings when we are in danger. The path of least resistance is the one toward which everyone naturally drifts. For the Christian, this tendency is to backslide into apathy, neglecting the life-changing truth of the gospel. The sacrificial life and death of Jesus destroyed the Devil's power over believers. Nothing should hold us back from the freedom of Christ.

The writer began the second chapter of Hebrews by reminding his audience of God's authority and righteous judgment. If the blessings and consequences were great for obedience or neglect of God's written Word, shared through intermediaries, how much more accountable are people to His personal presence through the incarnation of Jesus?

But the chapter didn't end with God as Judge—He is also Father. God's people have received an incredible gift that should never be taken for granted—salvation. They have been made part of God's family. The writer began explaining how and why Jesus came to save the children of God.

Jesus shared the human experience of being flesh and blood in order to defeat two enemies that have plagued every person in history. Living as a real person and dying for humanity, He declared victory over our worst adversary, the Devil, and our worst fear—death. That is the only way He could provide us a glorious relationship with a righteous Judge and loving Father. By sharing in our sufferings and death, He paid the penalty we owed but couldn't pay. By becoming human, He identifies with us in order to save us. He is, therefore, worthy of complete devotion and trust.

"WHEN WE BECOME PREOCCUPIED WITH LIFE TO THE EXTENT THAT WE HAVE LITTLE TIME TO DEVELOP OUR SPIRITUAL CORE, THEN DRIFTING IS INEVITABLE."

—David Jeremiah

➤ HEBREWS 2:1-3,14-18

1 We must, therefore, pay even more attention to what we have heard, so that we will not drift away.

2 For if the message spoken through angels was legally binding and every transgression and disobedience received a just punishment,

3 how will we escape if we neglect such a great salvation? It was first spoken by the Lord and was confirmed to us by those who heard Him.

_____

14 Now since the children have flesh and blood in common, Jesus also shared in these, so that through His death He might destroy the one holding the power of death —that is, the Devil—

15 and free those who were held in slavery all their lives by the fear of death.

16 For it is clear that He does not reach out to help angels, but to help Abraham's offspring.

17 Therefore, He had to be like His brothers in every way, so that He could become a merciful and faithful high priest in service to God, to make propitiation for the sins of the people.

18 For since He Himself was tested and has suffered, He is able to help those who are tested.

Think About It

What does the word "we" suggest about the relationship between the writer and the readers?

What situations cause a person to drift when it comes to obeying Christ?

What difference does it make that Jesus was one of us?

❯ EXPLORE THE TEXT

LISTEN *(Read Hebrews 2:1.)*

Establishing Jesus' absolute and undeniable authority, the writer of Hebrews issued a solemn warning to His readers. Their decision to give up on Christ and look for another path to God would have disastrous results. The first verse of Hebrews 2 addresses drifters. The writer of Hebrews issued a stern warning that needs careful attention.

A ship in a harbor, if not properly anchored, will follow the path of least resistance and drift away. In many ways, we're a lot like ships. Through spiritual neglect, by looking in the wrong direction, or by looking for what we think is an easier way, we end up where we never intended to be. When we get there, we feel miserable and may not even know why. Ultimately, we must be anchored in Christ.

Like the early believers, we also face the same temptation and the same warning. Instead of simply glancing at the gospel and then forgetting about it, we must give careful consideration to Christ in our lives.

How have you been tempted to let tough times have a negative impact on your faith in Christ?

Using the idea of a sailor paying close attention to the sea as he brought the ship toward the harbor, the writer of Hebrews warns all Christ followers to be alert and on guard as they make decisions about living out their confession of Christ.

What warning signs exist to help Christ followers avoid drifting away from Him?

THE PERIL OF NEGLECT *(Read Hebrews 2:2-3.)*

On Mount Sinai, God made a covenant with His people, and His law figured prominently into it. Every portion of it had to be taken seriously as a binding agreement between Him and them. Therefore, they couldn't alter it at their convenience. God would hold them accountable for disobeying Him. They expected Him to give them the punishment they deserved when, in their disobedience, they transgressed the law.

How does the binding nature of God's law affect your sense of accountability to Him?

The writer also directed his readers to the binding authority of the gospel message. Their commitment to Jesus had been based on the received message, so it couldn't be altered simply because they wanted to change it. Neither would it disappear over time. They couldn't escape the consequences if they drifted away from it.

Real life begins when we respond to the good news of Christ. That's why growing believers understand that nothing surpasses God's great gift of salvation through Christ. Our past, our present, and our future have been changed forever because we heard the message of salvation and placed our faith in Christ as a result. Instead of neglecting it, we live it out every day in ways that show how much we cherish it.

How do you demonstrate to others that the gospel of Christ is a cherished treasure in your life?

Bible Skill:
Dig deeper into the background and usage of key words or phrases

Focus on the phrase "make propitiation" in Hebrews 2:17. Look up the word "propitiation" in an English dictionary to discover its basic meaning. Then compare the phrase in several trusted Bible translations. Use a concordance to find other uses of the term in the Scriptures.

Like the angels served to bring about the law in the Old Testament, Christ had been responsible for bringing the message of salvation. Since Christ was God, then God Himself had proclaimed it, making it absolutely superior. Therefore, it had to be considered a precious treasure by the people who had been saved. They had been saved because they heard it and had received Christ.

Referring to *us*, the writer indicated that he and his readers shared the same testimony regarding the message of salvation. Neither the writer nor the readers had heard it from Jesus directly. Someone had shared the gospel with them and confirmed the message Jesus proclaimed. Therefore, it had the same binding authority as Jesus' first-hand proclamation.

When the gospel message was first spoken to you, how did you know you were hearing the truth?

TO DESTROY THE DEVIL
(Read Hebrews 2:14-16.)

Drawing attention to the humanity of Christ, the writer of Hebrews drove home the point that we can trust Jesus. He was the only sinless person to ever exist. Jesus didn't become a man so He could know us, prove anything to us, or convince us that He understood our condition. He had a redemptive purpose in mind—to save us. The manger, the cross, and the empty tomb demonstrate His intention to set us free.

Jesus gave Himself for us to deliver us from the grip of Satan. The Devil has always been portrayed as the adversary of God and His kingdom. In the Old Testament, he was called the accuser whom the

Lord rebuked (see Zech. 3:1-2). Jesus referred to Satan as a murderer from the beginning and a liar (see John 8:44). One of Jesus' disciples, Simon Peter, described the Devil as a roaring lion in search of prey to devour (see 1 Pet. 5:8). The Lord's life, death, and resurrection wiped out Satan's scheme to gain control.

Jesus also delivered us from the power of death. He set us free from spiritual slavery. Because of His resurrection, we no longer need to face death with terror. Instead, we understand that physical death gives way to eternal life in heaven with Him. In time, death will be destroyed (see 1 Cor. 15:54). We still face death, but through His sacrificial death, Jesus removed the sting of death that came as a result of sin. As Christians, we can face death with confidence and anticipation. Christ became human because we needed His help as sinners. If He had not taken on flesh and bones, we would still be under the control of Satan, dreading death, and without hope. His willingness to come to us and to die in our place points to His love for us.

Read Colossians 2:12-15 and 1 John 3:8. How do these verses explain Jesus' defeat of the Devil?

TESTED *(Read Hebrews 2:17-18.)*

In the days of the Old Testament, the high priest led in a special time of worship on the Day of

Atonement. During the service, the high priest would enter the holy of holies, a restricted section of the tabernacle or temple. Only the high priest could enter it, and only on the Day of Atonement (see Lev. 16:34; 23:27-28). Once inside the holy of holies, he would offer a blood sacrifice to cleanse his people of their sin.

Jesus serves as the perfect High Priest because He presented Himself to God in order to atone for our sin. On the cross, He also provided what was necessary for our atonement. By dying for us, Jesus made propitiation for our sins. In other words, His death on the cross for our sins turned away God's wrath so that we can be at peace with God. His death on the cross for us demonstrates that He is altogether trustworthy in His service to God on our behalf.

With verse 18, the writer of Hebrews pointed directly to the full extent of Jesus' humanity. Jesus didn't get special treatment because He was the Son of God. In fact, He got the opposite. In the wilderness, Satan confronted Jesus with an assortment of attractive temptations (see Matt. 4:1-11). Jesus overcame the Enemy's attack by quoting God's Word. Although the Devil left Jesus for a while, He repeatedly returned with relentless attacks. None can say that Jesus didn't know what it was like to be tempted and tried.

Jesus also suffered in unimaginable ways. Throughout His ministry, He lived under extreme pressures. He was the daily target of religious zealots, misguided relatives, needy disciples, and cruel critics. But nothing compared to the suffering He endured on the cross. He faced the physical, emotional, and spiritual anguish of it all without backing down one step.

Because of the temptations Jesus faced and the agony He suffered, He can empathize with any situation we may face. Christ-followers who struggle with persecution or the pains of life can lean on Him. Christ stands ready to help when we're tested by all kinds of painful dilemmas. In addition, He enables us to experience victory over the Enemy's attempt to defeat us. Indeed, Jesus Christ is our merciful and faithful high priest.

Key Doctrine: Evangelism

It is the duty of every Christian to win the lost to Christ through verbal witness reinforced by a godly lifestyle.

❯ OBEY THE TEXT

Believers must guard against drifting away from the truth of the gospel. We can have confidence in the validity of the gospel message.

What gives you the greatest confidence to stand boldly for Christ? Explain.

List ways your Bible study group can provide spiritual support to keep each other from drifting.

As hard as one may try, people aren't capable of breaking the power of sin on their own. We are in need of a Savior, but He must be one of us. Christ took on a human body to be that Savior.

What impact does Jesus' being one of us have on the way you pray about your temptations?

MEMORIZE

"We must, therefore, pay even more attention to what we have heard, so that we will not drift away" (Hebrews 2:1).

Use the space provided to make observations and record prayer requests during the group experience for this session.

MY THOUGHTS

Record insights and questions from the group experience.

_____

_____

_____

_____

_____

_____

MY RESPONSE

Note specific ways you will put into practice the truth explored this week.

_____

_____

_____

_____

_____

_____

MY PRAYERS

List specific prayer needs and answers to remember this week.

_____

_____

_____

_____

_____

_____

WATCH OUT!

Believers must encourage each other to firmly hold to Jesus.

❯ UNDERSTAND THE CONTEXT

PREPARE FOR YOUR GROUP EXPERIENCE WITH THE FOLLOWING PAGES.

At least some of the first readers of the Book of Hebrews were believers who came to Christ out of a background of Judaism. They were steeped in Old Testament understanding. When they heard the gospel, they believed in Jesus as Messiah and Lord.

Now, however, their confession of Christ had begun to prove costly. They encountered hostility and suffered hardships because of their faith. Therefore, some of them had stopped gathering with other believers for worship in fear of being identified and targeted as Christians. They showed signs of retreating from their confession of Christ.

From the very first words of his epistle, the writer of Hebrews urged these faltering believers to consider carefully who Jesus is. Jesus is the Divine Son of God (1:1-3) who vastly outranks the angels (1:4-14). Yet Jesus also took on human nature to provide a great salvation that must not be neglected (2:1-18).

The writer didn't discount the prophets, angels, Moses, or Old Testament worship and sacrifice. God had spoken through those means in the past. Yet they only foreshadowed what Jesus did by coming in the flesh, dying on the cross, and rising from the dead.

The writer used not only Old Testament imagery (3:1-6) but also quotations of Old Testament Scripture (3:7-11) to warn believers in his day not to be drawn into a state of fear and retreat. They needed to encourage one another daily to hold firmly to their confession of Jesus (3:12-19).

> "THE WORD THAT YOU FIND IN THE SCRIPTURE FROM GOD IS ALWAYS THE WORD 'TODAY'. THERE'S NEVER A 'TOMORROW'. THE ENEMY IS THE ONE WHO COMES AND TELLS US 'TOMORROW'. "
> —David Jeremiah

7 Therefore, as the Holy Spirit says: Today, if you hear His voice,

8 do not harden your hearts as in the rebellion, on the day of testing in the wilderness,

9 where your fathers tested Me, tried Me, and saw My works for 40 years.

10 Therefore I was provoked with that generation and said, "They always go astray in their hearts, and they have not known My ways."

11 So I swore in My anger, "They will not enter My rest."

12 Watch out, brothers, so that there won't be in any of you an evil, unbelieving heart that departs from the living God.

13 But encourage each other daily, while it is still called today, so that none of you is hardened by sin's deception.

14 For we have become companions of the Messiah if we hold firmly until the end the reality that we had at the start.

15 As it is said: Today, if you hear His voice, do not harden your hearts as in the rebellion.

Think About It

What do the phrases used in verses 7 and 15 indicate about the writer's view of Scripture?

Highlight the words and phrases in verses 12-15 that direct believers concerning what they are to do and not do.

❯ EXPLORE THE TEXT

KNOW YOUR HISTORY (Read Hebrews 3:7-11.)

A huge benefit Christians have in studying the Old Testament is to learn from the examples of ancient Israel (see 1 Cor. 10:1-6). The writer of Hebrews pointed to an unforgettable example: the Israelites' rebellion against God during their journey to the promised land. The historical account of this journey appears in Exodus and Numbers. However, the writer of Hebrews quoted not from the historical accounts but from Psalm 95. This was a psalm used in Jewish worship. It called for unflinching devotion to the Lord and warned against disobedience.

The writer introduced his quotation of Psalm 95:7-11 by stating that the Holy Spirit said it. This introduction has two purposes. First, it underscores the writer's view of Scripture. God is the ultimate Author of all Scripture. The Holy Spirit directed its various writers so that what we have today in the Bible is truly God's Word, not our own ideas about God (see 2 Tim. 3:16-17; 2 Pet. 1:20-21).

Second, it shows that believers of every generation can and should follow the spiritual guidance in all of Scripture. The Old and New Testaments are not two stories but one story of which Jesus is the center.

When you read Scripture, what helps you know that God is speaking to you through it?

The people had shown a stiff-necked spirit from the time they came out of Egypt until they camped on the edge of the promised land. They complained at the Red Sea (see Ex. 14:11-12). In the wilderness, they grumbled about a lack of water (see Ex. 15:24), a lack of food (see Ex. 16:2-3), and about hardships (see Num. 11:1). Rather than growing in their faith as God took care of them in every hardship, they drifted in their faith. They failed the test of faith by testing God. Their hearts grew distant, then hard, and finally disobedient. Their lack of

faith reached a tipping point when they refused to enter the promised land (see Num. 14:2-4,11-12).

Only two of Israel's leaders, Joshua and Caleb, stood boldly with Moses at that time and urged the people to move forward in faith. Consequently, only those two men of their generation were permitted to survive for 40 years of wilderness wanderings and to enter the promised land (see Num. 14:30-35).

How can difficult situations become times of significant spiritual growth?

God judged the disobedient Israelites by declaring they wouldn't enjoy a settled life in the promised land (see Josh. 21:43-45). The generation of Israelites who rebelled in the wilderness died in the wilderness. God didn't abandon them as His people, but they never enjoyed the full blessings of life God promised.

What blessings in life can we miss because of disobedience?

HEED THE WARNING *(Read Hebrews 3:12.)*

The believers addressed in Hebrews needed to pay attention to the example of the disobedient Israelites.

The hardships these Christians faced presented them with a moment of truth. Either they would trust God and endure in their confession of Jesus Christ or they would drift from God. The longer they drifted, the harder their hearts would become toward the promises of God. The more their lives would exhibit evil and unbelief rather than devotion and faith.

For this reason, the writer implored his readers to watch out. They were in danger of provoking God's wrath, just as the Israelites had done. If God judged His rebellious people in Old Testament times, He also will judge disobedient believers in New Testament times. The writer didn't want his readers to take a foolish direction in their journey of faith. He wanted them to turn back to the truth (see Jas. 5:19-20).

This same warning is relevant for believers today. We must not let unbelief have any place in our hearts. We need to be especially alert in times of hardship. Those are times when the Devil sows seeds of doubt in believers' minds. If we keep growing in our devotion to Christ, those seeds never germinate. If we drift in our faith, those seeds of doubt can quickly spring up into weeds of disobedience.

What seeds of doubt has the Devil thrown at you in times of hardship?

How do you resist those temptations?

Key Doctrine: Believers and Sin

Believers may fall into sin through neglect and temptation, where they grieve the Spirit and bring reproach on the cause of Christ and temporal judgment on themselves; yet they will be kept by the power of God through faith unto salvation.

ENCOURAGE EACH OTHER *(Read Hebrews 3:13-15.)*

As we follow Christ, we will face many situations that test our faith (see 2 Tim. 3:12; Jas. 1:2). God uses faithful believers as sources of encouragement for other believers (see 2 Cor. 1:3-4). We must not only take care of our own devotion to Christ but also do our best to watch out for our fellow believers.

A critical area for mutual encouragement involves our hearts. A believer's heart serves as the spiritual center of his or her life. As we obey His direction in our lives, our trusting hearts grow stronger in devotion to Christ. Strong devotion opens our spiritual ears to the truth. By contrast, a doubtful heart is open to deception. The deceived heart grows callous to God, and disobedience follows.

The Old Testament prophet Jeremiah warned that the heart is full of deceit (see Jer. 17:9). Avoiding sin's deception, therefore, involves keeping our hearts tender and open to God. A growing faith in Christ is every believer's best defense against temptation. We need to encourage one another daily to keep a tender heart of devotion to Christ.

The biblical writer gave us the reason for constantly nurturing a tender heart as believers. He explained that believers show they are fully devoted to Christ when they endure in their faith to the end. Enduring in faith is evidence of a full-fledged devotion to Christ, a devotion that endures no matter what hardships may come (see Rev. 2:10).

How has God worked through fellow Christ-followers to encourage you during difficult times?

Bible Skill:
Notice repeated words or phrases in a Bible passage.

Biblical writers sometimes used repetition of key words to emphasize a theme or message.

Identify the word used three times in Hebrews 3:7-15. (Hint: See vv. 7,13,15.)

Look also for the writer's use of similar, related words in the passage. (Hint: See vv. 8,13.)

What meaning does the repeated word have for Bible readers today?

❯ OBEY THE TEXT

If we trust in religious writings, religious leaders, or anything other than Christ for our salvation, we'll find ourselves deceived. Christ followers must encourage each other to remain faithful, reminding themselves and others that Christianity is a lifelong journey of faith.

What does it mean to you that your salvation in Christ is kept by God's power and not your own?

God's Word can encourage others in their spiritual walk. List a Bible verse you'll use this week to encourage another person.

MEMORIZE

"Encourage each other daily, while it is still called today" (Hebrews 3:13a).

Use the space provided to make observations and record prayer requests during the group experience for this session.

MY THOUGHTS
Record insights and questions from the group experience.

_____
_____
_____
_____
_____
_____

MY RESPONSE
Note specific ways you will put into practice the truth explored this week.

_____
_____
_____
_____
_____
_____

MY PRAYERS
List specific prayer needs and answers to remember this week.

_____
_____
_____
_____
_____
_____

SECURED WITH CONFIDENCE

Through His sacrifice, Jesus secured our salvation.

› UNDERSTAND THE CONTEXT

PREPARE FOR YOUR GROUP EXPERIENCE WITH THE
FOLLOWING PAGES.

The writer of Hebrews urged his readers to make every effort to
enter the "Sabbath rest" that God promised His people (4:9-11).
This rest is patterned after God's work in creation. In six days,
God created the universe and all within it; on the seventh day, He
rested. This rest was God's full enjoyment of and interaction with
all He had created. God blessed the seventh day and declared it
holy (see Gen. 2:1-3).

In Old Testament times, the Israelites observed weekly Sabbaths
as well as a few special Sabbaths throughout the year. One of
the most important was the Sabbath connected with the Day of
Atonement. On this one day each year the Israelite high priest
made an atoning offering before the Lord to cover the people's sins
(see Lev. 16:29-34).

Jesus' ministry as the Great High Priest is mentioned in the Book
of Hebrews as early as chapter 1, verse 3. There the writer spoke
of the Son having purged (or made purification for) sins. This was
a reference to Christ's death on the cross, the once-and-for-all
atoning sacrifice that only the Great High Priest could offer. In
2:17 and 3:1, the writer explained how the Son took on human
nature to identify fully with those He came to save. Then in 4:14–
5:10, the description of Jesus' ministry as High Priest comes into
full focus. Because of who Jesus is and what He did on the cross,
and because of His resurrection, Jesus' ministry as High Priest is
eternal. Rather than drifting from Christ, believers can confidently
approach the throne of grace at any time and for every need.

"THE OLD TESTAMENT
PRIEST WAS CHOSEN
FROM AMONG MEN
BECAUSE THEN HE
WOULD FEEL WHAT
OTHER MEN FELT."
—*David Jeremiah*

4:14 Therefore, since we have a great high priest who has passed through the heavens—Jesus the Son of God—let us hold fast to the confession.

15 For we do not have a high priest who is unable to sympathize with our weaknesses, but One who has been tested in every way as we are, yet without sin.

16 Therefore let us approach the throne of grace with boldness, so that we may receive mercy and find grace to help us at the proper time.

5:1 For every high priest taken from men is appointed in service to God for the people, to offer both gifts and sacrifices for sins.

2 He is able to deal gently with those who are ignorant and are going astray, since he is also subject to weakness.

3 Because of this, he must make a sin offering for himself as well as for the people.

4 No one takes this honor on himself; instead, a person is called by God, just as Aaron was.

5 In the same way, the Messiah did not exalt Himself to become a high priest, but the One who said to Him, You are My Son; today I have become Your Father,

6 also said in another passage, You are a priest forever in the order of Melchizedek.

Think About It

Identify two actions believers are urged to take as a result of Jesus' being the Great High Priest. (Hint: Look for the phrase "let us.")

How confident are you when you approach the Lord in prayer or in Bible study? When do you feel most confident? Least confident?

❯ EXPLORE THE TEXT

CONFIDENCE *(Read Hebrews 4:14-16.)*

If many of the first readers of Hebrews were former followers of Judaism, then they were well aware of the important role of the high priest. Until A.D. 70, when the Roman army sacked Jerusalem in response to a rebellion, the majestic temple stood at the center of Jewish life. The sacrificial system flourished, and thousands of priests longed for an assignment to serve at the temple in the holy city. The position of high priest also continued, although the actions of high priests such as Caiaphas and his father-in-law, Annas, proved that high priests in Jesus' day often cared more about their own political survival than about the people's spiritual condition. Such priests feared Rome more than they feared God (see John 11:48-50; 18:19-24; Acts 4:5-7,13-18).

The writer of Hebrews confessed that Jesus is of a higher order than all past or present high priests. Jesus is the Great High Priest. Just as He is the King of kings and the Lord of lords, Jesus also is the Priest of priests—the Great, or Ultimate, High Priest.

Jesus is our Great High Priest because He laid down His life on the cross as an atoning sacrifice for sinners. He arose from the dead in victory over sin and death. Earthly high priests lived, served, and then died. Jesus, however, lives forever to advocate for all who trust in Him for salvation (see Heb. 7:25). Earthly high priests entered the temple's most holy place to come before God. Jesus, however, entered directly into the presence of the Heavenly Father, sitting down at His right hand (see Heb. 1:3).

In what specific ways do others see you live out your confession of faith in Christ?

Jesus as our High Priest understands what it is like to be human, to face the limitations and weaknesses of our physical nature. He took on human nature when He came to earth as the child born of the virgin Mary. He laid aside His divine station and took on human flesh with all of its physical needs and weaknesses, including physical death (see Phil. 2:6-8). He experienced thirst, hunger, exhaustion, sorrow, disappointment, and anger.

Moreover, Jesus our Great High Priest experienced the powerful tug of temptation (see Matt. 4:1-11). He was tested, tried, and tempted in every way that we humans can be tempted—with one gigantic difference. Jesus never sinned! Not in thought, word, or deed. He never once failed to live in obedience to the Father. Even when horrible suffering and a brutal death on the cross drew near, Jesus prayed to the Father, "Not My will, but Yours, be done" (Luke 22:42).

When we look honestly in the mirror of God's Word, we become aware of our weaknesses—both physical and spiritual. But we can find strength in knowing that our Savior not only understands, but He is moved with compassion to help us. By His Spirit who lives in us, our Great High Priest strengthens us to resist temptation, just as He resisted in every situation.

How does knowing that Jesus faced and overcame all temptation help you resist temptations?

He understands what we're facing when we're tempted, and He knows what we need to escape the temptation (see 1 Cor. 10:13). In humble prayer, we can come into His presence with repentance ... and leave with forgiveness. We can lay our weakness at His feet ... and leave with His strength. We can approach Him in our time of need ... and leave with a superabundance of His mercy and grace.

What can cause a person to lose boldness to approach the Lord in prayer for help?

> **Key Doctrine: Jesus' Sinless Life**
>
> Jesus perfectly revealed and did the will of God, taking upon Himself human nature and identifying Himself completely with mankind yet without sin.

FOUND IN CHRIST *(Read Hebrews 5:1-6.)*

An earthly high priest was appointed from among the people to an important ministry. On the one hand, he served God by teaching His Word to the people. On the other hand, he represented the people before God by offering the various sacrifices, including sin offerings. A true and godly high priest took seriously his calling to be a servant of both God and God's people. He took seriously the matter of the people's sins because God took their sins seriously.

As the God-Man, Jesus also came from among the people. The writer of Hebrews declared it in 2:17 and implied it again here in 5:1. Yet he would also show in the coming verses that the similarities between earthly high priests and Jesus are overwhelmed by Jesus' greatness, or uniqueness.

A faithful and merciful high priest is able to deal gently with sinners because he knows that he too struggles with the weakness of the flesh.

In fact, every earthly high priest who approached God on the Day of Atonement first had to make an atonement offering for himself and his family (see Lev. 16:6-14).

How does knowing that Jesus sympathizes with your weaknesses help you approach the Father with your needs?

Again, Jesus' ministry was similar to that of an earthly high priest in that He understands our struggle with temptation. He was tested in similar ways, yet without yielding to sin (see Heb. 4:15). He too offered a sin offering. Yet His sacrifice was not for Him. He was the sin offering. He gave Himself on the cross that we might be made right with God through faith in Him (see 2 Cor. 5:21).

God called Aaron, Moses' brother, to be the first Israelite high priest (see Ex. 28:1). Yet Aaron committed a grievous sin by caving in to the Israelites' desire at Mount Sinai to create a golden calf idol (see Ex. 32:1-4). God mercifully forgave Aaron and allowed him to serve as high priest. The important point for the writer of Hebrews was that Aaron didn't take on the role of high priest by his own desire or moral qualifications. God called Aaron to serve. This truth still holds for those whom God calls into Christian service today. It isn't because of our qualifications; it's because of God's grace!

Jesus didn't grasp at the ministry of High Priest for self-glory. Rather, the Heavenly Father called the Son into this service on behalf of believers. Jesus serves forever as the believer's High Priest.

In this regard, the writer of Hebrews pointed to the biblical example of Melchizedek, a name meaning "my king is righteousness." Melchizedek appeared on the scene abruptly—and disappeared in like fashion—in the time of Abram, or Abraham (see Gen. 14:18-20). Identified as the king of Salem and a priest of God Most High, Melchizedek blessed Abraham after a military victory and received an offering from the grateful patriarch. In Psalm 110, King David mentioned Melchizedek as the type of priest the coming Messiah would be. The writer of Hebrews used the example of Melchizedek a number of times to reinforce Jesus' ministry as believers' Great High Priest (see Heb. 5:6,10; 6:20; 7:1-3,10, 11,15,17).

How does knowing that Jesus is our Great High Priest forever impact your prayer life?

Bible Skill:
Use a concordance and/or Bible dictionary to learn more about a feature of Israel's religious life.

Use a concordance to find references in Scripture to "high priest." Jot down your findings about the high priest's role and importance. List as many names as you can find of persons who served as high priest.

How does it impact your confidence in confessing Christ in a skeptical and sometimes hostile culture?

❯ OBEY THE TEXT

Christ makes it possible for humans to approach the Father with confidence. He knows our limits and deepest needs, and is ready to give us His grace and strength. By showing God's grace and mercy to others, we demonstrate Christ to a watching world.

What steps do you need to take to increase your confidence in Christ?

What hinders you from sympathizing with others when they share prayer needs?

What action can you take to show a greater concern for group members in need?

MEMORIZE

"Therefore let us approach the throne of grace with boldness, so that we may receive mercy and find grace to help us at the proper time" (Hebrews 4:16).

Use the space provided to make observations and record prayer requests during the group experience for this session.

MY THOUGHTS

Record insights and questions from the group experience.

_____
_____
_____
_____
_____
_____

MY RESPONSE

Note specific ways you will put into practice the truth explored this week.

_____
_____
_____
_____
_____
_____

MY PRAYERS

List specific prayer needs and answers to remember this week.

_____
_____
_____
_____
_____
_____

DON'T WALK AWAY

Rejecting Christ leads to hopelessness.

❯ UNDERSTAND THE CONTEXT

Hope doesn't come easily, and it doesn't last long if it's based solely on circumstances. That's because when things are going well in our lives, hope bubbles up and lingers. But when tough times come, our sense of hope fades away and sometimes disappears.

The biblical idea of hope is different. In Scripture, hope is something that endures. It endures because it's based on the eternal, living Lord and not on our circumstances. The theme of spiritual maturity in Christ takes center stage in the Book of Hebrews. If we press on toward maturity in Christ, we'll rejoice in the way He strengthens us. Those who fall away from devotion to Christ because of life's difficulties or because of opposition to the faith prove they need to grow in their faith or that they never have truly received salvation in Him.

The writer of Hebrews contended that by now his readers should have been much more mature in the faith than they were acting (see 5:11-14). He compared them to infants whose diet consists only of milk rather than solid food. Many were acting so spiritually immature they still needed to be fed only the "milk" of God's Word. In the writer's judgment, they should have been mature enough by that time to teach others. Instead, they were stuck in spiritual kindergarten, still in need of mastering the ABC's of the gospel.

The time had come for these believers to move on toward maturity in Christ. That's the urgent message the writer wanted to impress on those who were wavering in faith.

"MATURITY STARTS WITH A DECISION; A DECISION TO MAKE OUR GROWTH IN CHRIST A PRIORITY. WHILE WE ARE SAVED BY FAITH AND NOT BY WORKS, OUR GROWTH IN FAITH REQUIRES US TO BE INVOLVED IN THE PROCESS."
—*David Jeremiah*

➤ HEBREWS 6:1-8

1 Therefore, leaving the elementary message about the Messiah, let us go on to maturity, not laying again the foundation of repentance from dead works, faith in God,

2 teaching about ritual washings, laying on of hands, the resurrection of the dead, and eternal judgment.

3 And we will do this if God permits.

4 For it is impossible to renew to repentance those who were once enlightened, who tasted the heavenly gift, became companions with the Holy Spirit,

5 tasted God's good word and the powers of the coming age,

6 and who have fallen away, because, to their own harm, they are recrucifying the Son of God and holding Him up to contempt.

7 For ground that has drunk the rain that has often fallen on it and that produces vegetation useful to those it is cultivated for receives a blessing from God.

8 But if it produces thorns and thistles, it is worthless and about to be cursed, and will be burned at the end.

Think About It

Highlight six basic Christian beliefs mentioned in verses 1-2.

Read verses 4a (end with the word "enlightened") and 6 as one sentence. Take note of what is impossible and why.

❯ EXPLORE THE TEXT

GROW IN FAITH (Read Hebrews 6:1-3.)

The writer began this section with the word *therefore*. This word links the teachings in chapters 4 and 5 about Jesus as the Great High Priest with the writer's passionate warning against immaturity. To settle for an immature faith—whether out of spiritual laziness or fear—would be a disastrous choice for any believer to make.

Moreover, such a decision makes no sense. Believers have a Great High Priest in Jesus Christ. He is able to sympathize with our weaknesses. He Himself learned obedience to the Father through the sufferings He endured (see 5:8). Consequently, Jesus is the Source of help for all who follow Him. To drift away from one's confession of Christ is to starve the soul of the solid nourishment it craves.

We must not misunderstand what the writer meant in verse 1 by *leaving*, or moving beyond, the basic principles of the doctrine of Christ. He didn't mean to let go of the gospel in favor of some other set of beliefs. Rather, he meant that once someone has trusted in Christ for salvation, that believer is to grow spiritually, based on the truths already embraced. To leave the elementary teachings means to take the ABC's of the faith and to start threading together words, sentences, paragraphs, and chapters of obedient Christian living. The moment people receive Christ as Savior and Lord, they begin writing an ongoing story of their new life in Christ.

With the words *let us* in verse 1, the writer exhorted his readers as a fellow believer. He was a beloved Christian leader and teacher, yet he included himself among those who needed to keep pressing on toward spiritual maturity. The apostle Paul echoed this thought when he admitted that he too—although fully captured by Christ—hadn't yet reached the goal of full maturity. Every day, Paul put the past behind him and reached forward to what lay ahead (see Phil. 3:12-14). So should we.

The writer listed these six basic truths of the gospel as a foundation for our lives:

1. Repentance. Works-based religions insist that we have to earn our salvation by doing good deeds. The gospel declares that even our best deeds are dead. They have no power to undo our sinful nature. We must repent of—that is, turn away from—our sinful deeds. Moreover, we must repent of trusting in our own goodness.

2. Faith. Not faith in just anything, however, but faith in God. God was in Christ, the Bible says, reconciling the world to Himself (see 2 Cor. 5:19). In repentance we turn away from trust in self; in faith we turn to God, trusting in Jesus Christ as the One the Father sent to be the Savior of the world (see John 3:16-17).

How would you explain repentance and faith to a friend who doesn't know Christ?

3. Baptisms. This instruction may have been related to an understanding of believer's baptism. However, the plural form of the word suggests that the writer might have been referring to the cleansing rites that were part of the readers' background in Judaism. The instruction may have been a clarification between Christian baptism and Jewish rituals. From the earliest preaching of the gospel, baptism by immersion in water was presented as the initial act of obedience in the believer's confession of Christ as Lord (see Matt. 28:19; Acts 2:37-38; 8:36-38).

4. The laying on of hands. In the Book of Acts, this simple act of worship often was connected with the Holy Spirit's presence in and empowerment of believers (see Acts 6:6; 8:17; 13:3; 19:6; 28:8). In addition, the act was used in affirming the spiritual gifts and calling of church leaders (see 2 Tim. 1:6).

5. Resurrection of the dead. Because of Jesus' resurrection from the dead, Christians also live with the sure hope that in Him we will be resurrected (see 1 Cor. 15:20-22).

6. Eternal judgment. After death comes the judgment (see Heb. 9:27). We will all stand before the Lord in judgment one day. For believers, however, standing before Him in judgment will be a time of reward and blessing, an experience of honoring the One who has set all things right (see 1 Cor. 3:11-15).

As we obey Christ, God permits us to build our lives on the foundation of the gospel. We never want to neglect, drift off of, or walk away from the foundation. But neither are we to stay on the ground floor of faith. We are to grow, building on the gospel foundation toward a fully mature, Christlike life (see Eph. 4:14-16).

How are obedience and faith connected? What does obeying the Lord teach you about faith in Him?

> **Key Doctrine: Security in Jesus**
>
> All true believers endure to the end. Those whom God has accepted in Christ will never fall away from the state of grace, but shall persevere to the end.

LEST YOU WALK AWAY *(Read Hebrews 6:4-8.)*

These verses are among the most challenging to understand in the Book of Hebrews. Sincere Bible students arrive at different views about whether the verses describe an immature believer, a person who professes to be a believer but proves not to be, or a hypothetical example meant to show how unthinkable it is for believers to retreat from their confession of Christ. The verses build on the writer's exhortation in 6:1-3 to press on toward spiritual maturity.

The writer had warned his readers not to follow the example of the rebellious Israelites in Old Testament times (see 3:7-11). That generation of God's people had stood on the threshold of the promised land but refused to enter. They were afraid of the obstacles they faced in the land. They didn't trust God to keep His promises. Consequently, God didn't permit that generation to enter the land and receive the blessings He had in store for them. He didn't disown them or declare they never belonged to Him. Yet neither did He allow any of the disobedient ones to settle in the land. They died in the wilderness.

Now fast-forward to the New Testament age. Were some of the readers of Hebrews drifting dangerously close to a similar fate? Their lack of faith didn't involve a geographical promise but rather a promise of full and meaningful life in Christ (see John 10:10). They flirted with a return to Judaism, similar to the way the rebellious Israelites had talked about returning to Egypt (see Num. 14:3-4).

How does the description of the believer in verses 4b-5 compare to your understanding of what it means to be a Christ follower?

The writer explained what a retreat in faith implied. If it were possible for someone who had tasted the goodness of the gospel, had believed, and had enjoyed the blessings of salvation to fall away from it, then that person could never be renewed to repentance. Why not? Because the person's action would hold Jesus up to contempt. It would in effect (although not in reality) put Jesus back on the cross instead of reigning as the victorious, resurrected Lord.

God blesses those who press on in faith toward spiritual maturity. Our bold confession of Christ even in the face of opposition or challenge demonstrates the reality of our faith. It's the evidence of genuine salvation.

Bible Skill: Use multiple Scripture passages to understand a major doctrine.

The question of whether a genuine believer can lose his or her salvation goes to the heart of the doctrine of salvation. Read the following Bible passages and take note of what they teach about salvation in Jesus: John 10:27-29; Romans 8:1,38-39; Ephesians 1:13-14; Philippians 1:6; 1 Peter 1:5.

How can you relate these passages to Hebrews 6:4-6?

❯ OBEY THE TEXT

Believers must be diligent to demonstrate their salvation, ever moving toward greater maturity. Mature believers can warn others of the dangers of immaturity and disobedience. Believers can help one another understand that Christianity is a lifelong faith commitment that grows and produces spiritual fruit.

What specific actions do you need to take toward strengthening your relationship with Christ? Who can help you be accountable for taking that action this week?

How can you warn someone about the dangers of failing to grow spiritually without sounding judgmental or superior?

How can you challenge other believers to build on the foundation of their faith? What role can you play in helping others mature in faith and produce spiritual fruit?

MEMORIZE

"Therefore, leaving the elementary message about the Messiah, let us go on to maturity" (Hebrews 6:1a).

Use the space provided to make observations and record prayer requests during the group experience for this session.

MY THOUGHTS
Record insights and questions from the group experience.

_____
_____
_____
_____
_____
_____

MY RESPONSE
Note specific ways you will put into practice the truth explored this week.

_____
_____
_____
_____
_____
_____

MY PRAYERS
List specific prayer needs and answers to remember this week.

_____
_____
_____
_____
_____
_____

ONLY JESUS SAVES

Jesus is the only One able to save us.

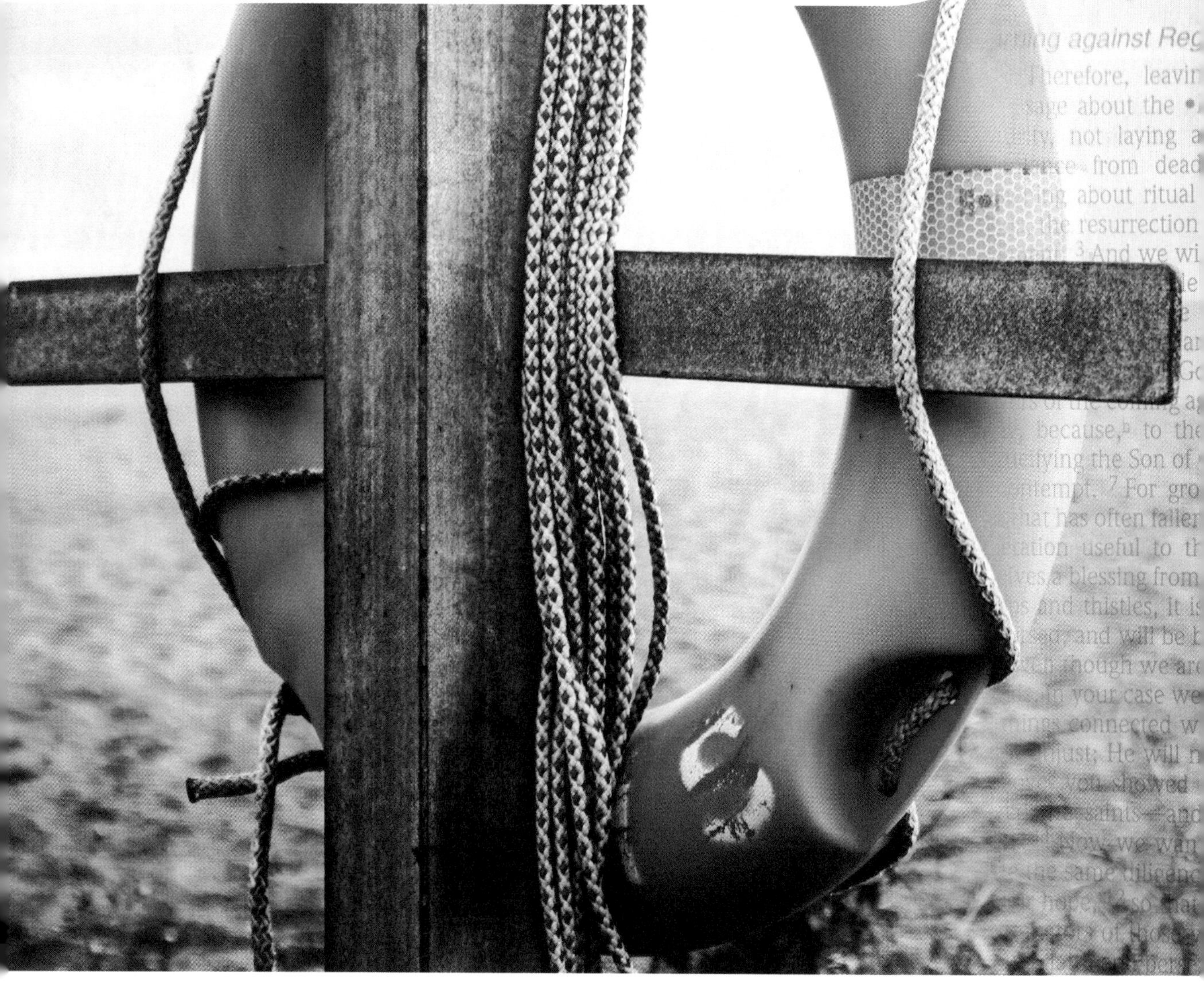

❯ UNDERSTAND THE CONTEXT

PREPARE FOR YOUR GROUP EXPERIENCE WITH THE FOLLOWING PAGES.

For the writer of Hebrews, Abraham was a case study of one whose faith and actions in Old Testament times pointed to Jesus' superiority as the believer's High Priest. God made a promise of descendants to Abraham and guaranteed it with an oath. Abraham found that God kept His promise. God made a promise that Jesus' ministry as High Priest would be similar in type to that of the Old Testament priest Melchizedek (see 6:13-20). The writer went into rich detail as he explained the ways that the ministry of Melchizedek foreshadowed Jesus' ministry as High Priest for believers (see 7:1-10).

Drawing from Genesis 14:18-20 and Psalm 110:4, the writer described Melchizedek as a priest of God Most High. He was also the king of Salem, a name meaning "peace." Scripture provides no genealogy for Melchizedek, and for this reason he foreshadowed the eternal nature of Jesus. In addition, Abraham gave a tithe offering to God through Melchizedek, an act that preceded the Levitical priesthood by hundreds of years. Thus, Melchizedek represented a prior and superior priesthood to that represented in Judaism. He foreshadowed the ministry of Jesus as the believer's Great High Priest.

Thus for a believing Jew to return to Judaism was to go back to an inferior priesthood. The writer then made a carefully reasoned argument concerning the uniqueness and superiority of Jesus' ministry as High Priest (see 7:11-28). Similar to the ministry of Melchizedek, Jesus' ministry as High Priest wasn't based on the law of Moses but on the power of an indestructible life. Therefore, Jesus established in Himself a new and better covenant. He is the Great High Priest to which the law of Moses could only point.

> "SINCE JESUS IS OUR HIGH PRIEST AND HE NEVER GOES AWAY AND HE NEVER CHANGES, HE'S ABLE TO SHEPHERD US ALL THE WAY HOME TO GLORY. NO OTHER PRIEST WILL EVER BE NECESSARY."
> —David Jeremiah

23 Now many have become Levitical priests, since they are prevented by death from remaining in office.

24 But because He remains forever, He holds His priesthood permanently

25 Therefore, He is always able to save those who come to God through Him, since He always lives to intercede for them.

26 For this is the kind of high priest we need: holy, innocent, undefiled, separated from sinners, and exalted above the heavens.

27 He doesn't need to offer sacrifices every day, as high priests do—first for their own sins, then for those of the people. He did this once for all when He offered Himself.

28 For the law appoints as high priests men who are weak, but the promise of the oath, which came after the law, appoints a Son, who has been perfected forever.

Think About It

When the word "but" appears in a sentence, it usually sets up a contrast between two or more things. Find the two instances of the word in these verses. Take note of what is contrasted in each instance.

› EXPLORE THE TEXT

A PERMANENT PRIEST (Read Hebrews 7:23-24.)

The writer of Hebrews sought to describe Jesus as Great High Priest. In these verses, he continued by explaining that Jesus was superior to the Levitical priests. They had their beginning with Aaron, Moses' brother. When the Israelites were camped at Mount Sinai, God appointed Aaron to be the first priest (see Ex. 28:1). After Aaron died, his son, Eleazar, replaced him and became the next priest over Israel (see Deut. 10:6). The priesthood continued throughout Old Testament times and was still in existence during the time of the New Testament. Each of the priests shared the same human limitation. Being a high priest did not protect a person from facing death. When a priest died, the ministry passed to someone else.

How would you describe the limits faced by a Jewish priest? How does each limit point to the need for a better priest?

In contrast to the Levitical priests who served and died, Jesus stood alone, and for an important reason. Jesus Christ is eternal. That uniqueness made Him superior to any earthly high priest. Jesus would never have to allow His priesthood to be passed on to anyone else.

For Christians today, the certainty of Jesus' unending relationship with us as our eternal High Priest gives us the rich assurance of His never-ending ministry in our lives. When we study God's Word, He will make Himself known in the pages of Scripture. We can turn to Him for help through tough times brought on by opposition to the gospel or by our weakness against temptation. When we think about the future, we don't need to be afraid, because we live in the certainty that He'll be there as well. He'll never be absent, and He'll never be replaced.

When you think about Jesus as your Great High Priest, what assurances does that reality give you?

ABLE TO SAVE *(Read Hebrews 7:25.)*

With his confident assertions about Jesus, the writer of Hebrews gives us a striking declaration. Jesus stands out as our eternal High Priest forever. Therefore, we can always live in complete confidence that the way to a right relationship with God will never change. No matter how many centuries pass or how many shifts in culture take place, Jesus will always stand alone as the centerpiece of the gospel. He will never be removed from His place of prominence, because He alone has the power to give the gift of eternal life. Because He died on the cross and rose from the dead to live eternally, He's able to save anyone who turns to Him.

When we think about being saved, we benefit from the big picture. That's the only way we can see how far and wide His salvation extends in our lives. To be saved means that we've received God's gift of salvation and have been rescued from the bondage of sin. We welcomed Christ into our lives when we repented of our sins and placed our complete faith in Him. When He gave us new life, He changed everything for us. Through Him, we began a personal walk of faith with God.

Being saved also means growing in our relationship with God. We never lose sight of the sublime reality that He loves us as His children. Because He loves us, He guides us to grasp His purpose and empowers us to live it out for His glory. Doing so gives us unparalleled contentment in Him.

Being saved also has a future dimension. It means that we look forward to being in heaven one day with God and with all believers. We can't earn a home in heaven by our works. Jesus is preparing that place for those who trust in Him (see John 14:1-3). Therefore, we can rest assured that heaven will be our eternal home.

All of these blessings of salvation come our way as Christians, because Jesus lives eternally to intercede for us. Seated at the right hand of the Heavenly Father, Jesus forever advocates for believers on the basis of His sinless life, atoning death, and victorious resurrection. He has done everything necessary to satisfy God's wrath against sin, to break sin's curse on humanity, and to provide the way of salvation.

As Christ lives in us as believers through the Holy Spirit, He provides everything we need so that we can grow into spiritually mature followers. We never have to wonder if someone or something else still needs to come along and advocate for our salvation. Christ intercedes for us perfectly and eternally today, tomorrow, and forever.

Do you view Jesus' being the only way of salvation as limiting or freeing? Explain.

Key Doctrine: Our Substitute

Jesus honored the divine law by His personal obedience, and in His substitutionary death on the cross He made provision for the redemption of people from sin.

BECAUSE OF HIS CHARACTER *(Read Hebrews 7:26-28.)*

Jesus meets every need in our relationship with God, because He stands alone as our Great High Priest. His unique qualifications place Him high above anything or anyone else who might attempt to fulfill that role. He is holy, completely unique. There's no one like Him, because He's perfectly righteous.

Although He identified with us by taking on human nature, He's different from us in that He never sinned. He lived in the flesh for a short time, but now He is in heaven, having ascended from the earth after His resurrection (see Acts 1:9). He was and is exalted forever.

In your own words, how would you declare that Jesus is the High Priest you need?

Jesus doesn't need to make any more sacrifices. God required earthly priests to offer sacrifices for their own sins before they could offer sacrifices for others' sins (see Lev. 4:3; 16:6). However, by laying down His life for us on the cross, Jesus provided the perfect sin sacrifice once and for all.

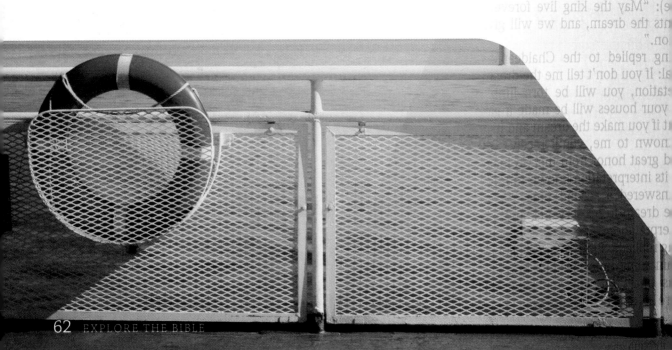

How can you express your gratitude to Christ for giving Himself as the Sacrifice to secure your salvation?

The writer of Hebrews concluded by making a comparison between the law and God's promise. A law might be repealed or changed, but an oath of promise could never be erased or altered. The contrast between the law's requirement and God's promise draws believers to a rock-solid certainty. Instead of being mortal like earthly priests, Jesus lives eternally. He will never die.

How would you explain to a friend that only Jesus is qualified to provide salvation?

Bible Skill: Create a compare/contrast chart to study a passage.

Using the space below, or on one side of a vertical line, list words and phrases that describe earthly priests. On the other side list words and phrases that describe Jesus the Son as High Priest. Use the chart to study Hebrews 7:11-28.

EARTHLY PRIEST

JESUS THE GREAT HIGH PRIEST

❯ OBEY THE TEXT

Only Jesus is qualified to save sinners from sin, death, and hell. Since salvation is based on Jesus' sinless life, atoning death, and victorious resurrection, those who believe in Him can live faithfully and share the gospel with confidence.

In what or whom are you trusting your life? Spend time this week examining your answer to this question. If you've never embraced Christ's salvation, talk with your Bible study leader or someone in your group.

With whom have you shared the gospel recently? How can you use this week's study to tell someone about salvation in Jesus?

Identify your biggest fears when it comes to sharing with others about Jesus. How does this passage address those fears? What action can you take this week to overcome one of your fears?

MEMORIZE

"Therefore, He is always able to save those who come to God through Him, since He always lives to intercede for them" (Hebrews 7:25).

Use the space provided to make observations and record prayer requests during the group experience for this session.

MY THOUGHTS

Record insights and questions from the group experience.

_____
_____
_____
_____
_____
_____

MY RESPONSE

Note specific ways you will put into practice the truth explored this week.

_____
_____
_____
_____
_____
_____

MY PRAYERS

List specific prayer needs and answers to remember this week.

_____
_____
_____
_____
_____
_____

> ## GETTING STARTED

OPENING OPTIONS: **Choose one of the following to open your group discussion:**

WEEKLY QUOTE DISCUSSION-STARTER: "Never has the biblical Jesus been dragged through the mud like He is in this current culture." —DAVID JEREMIAH

> › What is your initial response to this week's quote?

> › How have you experienced tension regarding others' perception of Jesus?

CREATIVE ACTIVITY: Prior to the group gathering, print off 3-5 images depicting Jesus Christ. These could be paintings, movie posters, biblical illustrations, and so on. (Note: color images will work best, if possible.) Display the images in a way that will be visible to group members during the meeting. Use the following questions to launch the group discussion:

> › What are your emotional reactions to these images?

> › Which image best characterizes Jesus in your mind? Why?

> ## UNDERSTAND THE CONTEXT

PROVIDE BACKGROUND: Briefly introduce group members to the Book of Hebrews by pointing out the major themes and any information or ideas that will help your group members explore Hebrews 1:1-4, specifically. Then, to personally connect today's context with the original context, ask the following questions:

> › Why would first century Christians be tempted to turn away from their faith in Jesus?

> › What does persecution look like in today's culture?

> › How are you tempted to compromise or abandon what you believe about Jesus?

❯ EXPLORE THE TEXT

READ THE BIBLE: Ask for a volunteer to read aloud Hebrews 1:1-4.

DISCUSS: Use the following questions to unpack your group members' initial reactions to the text.

> What do you like best about these verses? What questions do you have?

> What does God's communication reveal about His character?

> What specific descriptions are used for Jesus? How do they affect the way you view a relationship with Him?

> How do these opening verses encourage faithfulness and perseverance?

NOTE: Provide ample time for group members to share responses and questions regarding the text. Don't feel pressured to prioritize the printed agenda over your group members' personal experiences. If time allows, discuss responses to the questions in the reading.

❯ OBEY THE TEXT

RESPOND: Foster an environment of openness and action. Help individuals apply biblical truth to specific areas of personal thought, attitude, and/or behavior.

> How is God's Word challenging you right now?

> In what way will you keep this picture of Jesus in the forefront of your mind this week, especially when needing motivation to persevere through difficult situations?

> Who in your life needs to experience what you are learning? (Commit to pray for opportunities to share with him/her.)

PRAY: Conclude with prayer. Use the descriptors applied to Jesus in Hebrews 1:1-4 to guide your prayers, and conclude the experience by thanking God for revealing Himself through His Son.

For helps on how to use *Explore The Bible*, tips on how to better lead groups, or additional ideas for leading, visit: **www.ministrygrid.com/web/ExploreTheBible.**

❯ GETTING STARTED

OPENING OPTIONS: Choose one of the following to open your group discussion:

WEEKLY QUOTE DISCUSSION-STARTER: "When we become preoccupied with life to the extent that we have little time to develop our spiritual core, then drifting is inevitable." —DAVID JEREMIAH

> ❯ What is your initial response to this week's quote?

> ❯ How, specifically, has busyness affected your relationship with God and confidence in Him?

CREATIVE ACTIVITY: Call out a category and have people group themselves according to things they have in common. After groups have formed, have people reveal their answers and then call out a new category. Repeat this process a few times—ask at least one "revealing" question about opinion or personality. Examples of common bonds are: birth month, gender, favorite team, school or year of graduation, favorite show, favorite hobby, greatest fear. Use the following questions to launch the group discussion:

> ❯ What did you learn about someone in the group?

> ❯ How and why do we naturally gravitate toward people who have things in common with us?

> ❯ Why is it important to know that Jesus fully shared the human experience and understands us in every way?

❯ UNDERSTAND THE CONTEXT

PROVIDE BACKGROUND: Briefly introduce group members to any information or ideas that will help everyone explore Hebrews 2:1-3,14-18. Then, to personally connect today's context with the original context, ask the following questions:

> ❯ Why might the original audience have needed to be reminded of God's authority and righteous judgment?

> ❯ How do we tend to forget God's authority and judgment today?

⟩ EXPLORE THE TEXT

READ THE BIBLE: Ask for a volunteer to read aloud Hebrews 2:1-3,14-18.

DISCUSS: Use the following questions to unpack your group members' initial reactions to the text.

> What do you like best about these verses? What questions do you have?

> How is God's holiness revealed in these verses? His grace?

> What verbs are used in verses 1-3 for what we must do and what are the implications?

> What verbs are used in verses 14-18 for what Jesus has done and what are the implications?

> How do verses 14-18 explain our "great salvation" and what does it mean to neglect it?

NOTE: Provide ample time for group members to share responses and questions regarding the text. Don't feel pressured to prioritize the printed agenda over your group members' personal experiences. If time allows, discuss responses to the questions in the reading.

⟩ OBEY THE TEXT

RESPOND: Foster an environment of openness and action. Help individuals apply biblical truth to specific areas of personal thought, attitude, and/or behavior.

> In what circumstances are you most encouraged, knowing that Jesus both understands and frees you from them?

> How will you heed the warning against drifting and neglecting our great salvation this week?

PRAY: Conclude with prayer. Use the warning and encouragement from Hebrews 2 to guide your prayer. Specifically pray for spiritual focus and help in remembering that Jesus perfectly identifies with us and has overcome sin and temptation, fear and death. Pray for confidence to live fully in the freedom Christ provides.

❯ GETTING STARTED

OPENING OPTIONS: Choose one of the following to open your group discussion:

WEEKLY QUOTE DISCUSSION-STARTER: "The word that you find in the Scripture from God is always the word 'today.' There's never a 'tomorrow.' The Enemy is the one who comes and tells us 'tomorrow.'"—DAVID JEREMIAH

> ❯ What is your initial response to this week's quote?

> ❯ Where do you most often procrastinate?

> ❯ How is spiritual procrastination a dangerous or foolish habit?

CREATIVE ACTIVITY: Instruct group members to stand in a line in the middle of the room. Number people 1-2-1-2... Explain that everyone will need to respond to a series of movements but the 1s will cover their eyes and 2s will cover their ears and hum quietly. Without sight or hearing, have everyone respond to a series of at least 10 steps as you quickly call them out. For example: Step right. Step right. Step back. Step left... After at least 10 steps, have everyone open their eyes and sit back down. Use the following questions to begin discussion:

> ❯ What were the challenges of both: not hearing and not seeing? How did you try to focus?

> ❯ At any point did anything distract your attention from what I was asking you to do? Other noises? Concerns? Other people?

> ❯ In what ways do you struggle hearing or seeing God and responding to His Word? How have you felt out of sync with God and/or with others?

❯ UNDERSTAND THE CONTEXT

PROVIDE BACKGROUND: Briefly introduce group members to any information or ideas that will help everyone explore Hebrews 3:7-15. Then, to personally connect today's context with the original context, ask the following questions:

> ❯ Why is it important to understand the Jewish background of the earliest Christians to whom the Book of Hebrews was written?

> ❯ How would knowing someone's background or beliefs help you share the gospel today?

❯ EXPLORE THE TEXT

READ THE BIBLE: Ask for a volunteer to read aloud Hebrews 3:7-15.

DISCUSS: Use the following questions to unpack your group members' initial reactions to the text.

> ❯ What do you like best about these verses? What questions do you have?

> ❯ How does sin deceive us?

> ❯ Verse 8 encourages us not to harden our hearts—verse 13 warns against sin hardening our hearts. How are people actively involved in and responsible for guarding their hearts, instead of being helpless victims?

> ❯ What hope does this passage point to for Christ followers?

NOTE: Provide ample time for group members to share responses and questions regarding the text. Don't feel pressured to prioritize the printed agenda over your group members' personal experiences. If time allows, discuss responses to the questions in the reading.

❯ OBEY THE TEXT

RESPOND: Foster an environment of openness and action. Help individuals apply biblical truth to specific areas of personal thought, attitude, and/or behavior.

> ❯ How are you encouraged, knowing that Scripture (Old Testament and New Testament) speaks to you, thousands of years after it was first written?

> ❯ How have you been hard-hearted in the past—when have you disobeyed or delayed obedience?

> ❯ What is the Holy Spirit saying to you right now through His Word?

> ❯ "Today," what do you need to do to respond to what the Holy Spirit is saying to you?

> ❯ Who will you encourage daily to keep an open heart? Who will encourage you? Commit to regularly connecting with that person to encourage daily obedience to God.

PRAY: Conclude with prayer. Pray for each person specifically and/or encourage people to pair up and pray for one another. Pray for openness and responsiveness to the Holy Spirit every day this week.

> GETTING STARTED

OPENING OPTIONS: Choose one of the following to open your group discussion:

WEEKLY QUOTE DISCUSSION-STARTER: "The Old Testament priest was chosen from among men because then he would feel what other men felt." —DAVID JEREMIAH

> What is your initial response to this week's quote?

> How would your relationship with God be different if you kept in mind that Jesus completely understands and empathizes with you?

CREATIVE ACTIVITY: Prior to the group gathering, gather a few common objects of various textures. Place the items in a box, sock, or container where the items can be felt but not seen. Pass the container around, instructing everyone to feel the items without looking at them and when they know what something is, to pass the container to the next person. After everyone has felt the items, use the following questions to launch the group discussion:

> What were you able to identify, knowing what it felt like?

> Why is it comforting to know that Jesus knows you well enough to identify exactly what you're going through—no guessing or wondering—since He has experienced it all?

> UNDERSTAND THE CONTEXT

PROVIDE BACKGROUND: Briefly introduce group members to any information or ideas that will help everyone explore Hebrews 4:14–5:6. Then, to personally connect today's context with the original context, ask the following questions:

> What was the origin and purpose of Sabbath?

> When do we take time out of our schedules today to rest in God?

> How does Sabbath rest demonstrate confidence that God is in control?

❯ EXPLORE THE TEXT

READ THE BIBLE: Ask for a volunteer to read aloud Hebrews 4:14–5:6.

DISCUSS: Use the following questions to unpack your group members' initial reactions to the text.

> ❯ What do you like best about these verses? What questions do you have?

> ❯ What is mercy? Grace?

> ❯ What does the phrase "to help us at the proper time" reveal about God and our relationship with Him (4:16)?

> ❯ Why is the perfection of Christ important? The humility of Christ? The full humanity of Christ? The eternal nature of Christ?

NOTE: Provide ample time for group members to share responses and questions regarding the text. Don't feel pressured to prioritize the printed agenda over your group members' personal experiences. If time allows, discuss responses to the questions in the reading.

❯ OBEY THE TEXT

RESPOND: Foster an environment of openness and action. Help individuals apply biblical truth to specific areas of personal thought, attitude, and/or behavior.

> ❯ How have you experienced God's help "at the proper time" in your life (4:16)?

> ❯ In what specific areas do you need God's grace and mercy?

> ❯ How will you "approach the throne of grace with boldness" this week (4:16)?

PRAY: Conclude with prayer. Provide a time for everyone to voice a prayer, thanking God for His grace, mercy, sovereignty, and presence in their lives. Encourage group members to boldly request God's help in specific situations.

❯ GETTING STARTED

OPENING OPTIONS: Choose one of the following to open your group discussion:

WEEKLY QUOTE DISCUSSION-STARTER: "Maturity starts with a decision; a decision to make our growth in Christ a priority. While we are saved by faith and not by works, our growth in faith requires us to be involved in the process." —DAVID JEREMIAH

> ❯ What is your initial response to this week's quote?

> ❯ What is one specific way you have experienced growth as a child of God?

CREATIVE ACTIVITY: Provide a small tube of toothpaste or ketchup packet and a plate or bowl to a volunteer from your group. Instruct the volunteer to completely squeeze out the contents onto the surface provided. After they have emptied the tube or packet, direct them to now put everything back into the tube or packet. Allow a moment for the person to try their best, if they are willing, before using the following questions to begin discussion:

> ❯ When have you done or experienced something that couldn't be taken back and undone? (Responses can be funny or serious.)

> ❯ Fortunately we serve a patient and forgiving God, but when life is over our decisions can't be undone. How does it shape your perspective knowing that this life is the only one you get— when it's done, it's done?

❯ UNDERSTAND THE CONTEXT

PROVIDE BACKGROUND: Briefly introduce group members to any information or ideas that will help everyone explore Hebrews 6:1-8. Then, to personally connect today's context with the original context, ask the following questions:

> ❯ How does the biblical idea of hope differ from a worldly and circumstantial understanding?

> ❯ How is a hope that is dependent upon circumstances an indicator of spiritual immaturity?

❯ EXPLORE THE TEXT

READ THE BIBLE: Ask for a volunteer to read aloud Hebrews 6:1-8.

DISCUSS: Use the following questions to unpack your group members' initial reactions to the text.

> ❯ What do you like best about these verses? What questions do you have?

> ❯ How does religious behavior not always indicate spiritual growth or maturity?

> ❯ What do these verses reveal about obedience, fruit, and spiritual life?

> ❯ Which warning is more sobering and why: verses 1-3 or 4-8?

> ❯ What does it mean to be "recrucifying the Son of God," as warned against in verse 6?

> ❯ In the midst of warnings, how is the goodness of God woven throughout these verses?

NOTE: Provide ample time for group members to share responses and questions regarding the text. Don't feel pressured to prioritize the printed agenda over your group members' personal experiences. If time allows, discuss responses to the questions in the reading.

❯ OBEY THE TEXT

RESPOND: Foster an environment of openness and action. Help individuals apply biblical truth to specific areas of personal thought, attitude, and/or behavior.

> ❯ How has your spiritual growth been stagnant, producing "thorns and thistles," or have you been "recrucifying the Son of God" in apathy, active rebellion, or stubborn sin?

> ❯ Even though we never fully graduate, what will you do starting this week to leave an "elementary" understanding and grow up to spiritually mature living?

PRAY: Conclude with prayer. Ask for the Spirit's deep conviction within everyone's hearts— revealing areas of immaturity or even vain attempts to recrucify Christ. Pray for commitment to spiritual growth and active steps toward maturity.

❯ GETTING STARTED

OPENING OPTIONS: Choose one of the following to open your group discussion:

WEEKLY QUOTE DISCUSSION-STARTER: "Since Jesus is our High Priest and He never goes away and He never changes, He's able to shepherd us all the way home to glory. No other priest will ever be necessary." —DAVID JEREMIAH

> ❯ What is your initial response to this week's quote?

> ❯ What is most comforting to you and why: Jesus never goes away nor changes? Jesus is able to care for and lead us in this life and the next? We have an eternal home in glory? No other person needs to intercede for us to have a relationship with God?

CREATIVE ACTIVITY: Prior to the group gathering, save or print 3-5 images depicting seemingly permanent things that have changed over time. For example: a river has carved the Grand Canyon, the Statue of Liberty was not always green, the Sphinx used to have a nose, some local landmark or trend that has changed in your own community. Display the images and use the following questions to launch the group discussion:

> ❯ How have these things changed over time even though they seem(ed) permanent?

> ❯ What are some things you wish would never change? What do you wish would change?

> ❯ Why is it important to know that Jesus is perfect and His work on the cross has forever accomplished our salvation?

❯ UNDERSTAND THE CONTEXT

PROVIDE BACKGROUND: Briefly introduce group members to the major themes and any information or ideas that will help your group members explore Hebrews 7:23-28, specifically. Then, to personally connect with the original context, ask the following questions:

> ❯ What was the role of High Priest in biblical times?

> ❯ What leadership roles exist today among God's people? How are those roles similar to the priesthood? How are they different?

❯ EXPLORE THE TEXT

READ THE BIBLE: Ask for a volunteer to read aloud Hebrews 7:23-28.

DISCUSS: Use the following questions to unpack your group members' initial reactions to the text.

> What do you like best about these verses? What questions do you have?

> How is Jesus unlike any human to ever live, including other great spiritual leaders?

> What does it mean for Jesus to "save those who come to God through Him" and "to intercede" on their behalf (v. 25)?

> Why do all people need salvation and someone who can intercede for them?

NOTE: Provide ample time for group members to share responses and questions regarding the text. Don't feel pressured to prioritize the printed agenda over your group members' personal experiences. If time allows, discuss responses to the questions in the reading.

❯ OBEY THE TEXT

RESPOND: Foster an environment of openness and action. Help individuals apply biblical truth to specific areas of personal thought, attitude, and/or behavior.

> How do you need Jesus to intercede on your behalf right now?

> Who do you know that needs to experience the salvation and intercession of Jesus? Identify a specific person(s).

> What will you tell that person(s) this week about the salvation found only in Jesus?

PRAY: Conclude with prayer. Spend time first thanking God for saving each of you. Next pray for the salvation of people you know and love. Pray for a heart of compassion and urgency in sharing the life-changing good news of the gospel. Pray for continued spiritual growth, seeking to live out the things being learned through time together in God's Word.

❯TIPS FOR LEADING A GROUP

PRAYERFULLY PREPARE:

Prepare for each meeting by …

> **reviewing the weekly material and leader guide questions ahead of time.**

> **praying for each person in the group.**

Ask the Holy Spirit to work through you and the group discussion as you point to Jesus each week through God's Word.

MINIMIZE DISTRACTIONS:

Create an environment that is comfortable. Someone who is uncomfortable will be distracted and therefore not engaged in the group experience. Plan ahead, taking into consideration the following:

> **seating**

> **temperature**

> **lighting**

> **food or drink**

> **surrounding noise**

> **and general cleanliness (put pets away if meeting in a home)**

At best, thoughtfulness and hospitality shows guests and group members that they are welcomed and valued in whatever environment you choose to gather.

At worst, people may never notice your effort, but they are also not distracted. Everything in your ability should be done to help people focus on what is of greatest importance: connecting with God and with community.

INCLUDE OTHERS:

Your goal is to foster a community where people are welcomed just as they are, but encouraged to grow spiritually. Always be aware of opportunities to …

> **invite** new people to join your group.

> **include** any people who visit the group.

An inexpensive way to make first-time guests feel welcome or to invite someone to get involved is to give them a copy of your Bible study book.

ENCOURAGE DISCUSSION:

A good small group experience is one where …

- › **everyone participates.** Encourage everyone to ask questions, share responses, or read aloud.

- › **no one dominates—not even the leader.** Be sure that your time speaking as a leader takes up less than half of your time together as a group. Politely guide discussion if anyone dominates.

- › **nobody is rushed through questions.** Don't feel that a moment of silence is a bad thing—people often need time to think about their responses to questions they've just heard or to work up the courage to share what God is stirring in their hearts.

- › **input is affirmed and followed-up.** Make sure you point out something true or helpful in a response. Don't just move on. Build community with follow-up questions, asking how other people have experienced similar things or how a truth has shaped their understanding of God and the Scripture you are studying. People are less likely to speak up if they fear that you don't actually want to hear their answers or that you are only looking for a certain right answer.

- › **God and His Word are central.** Opinions and experiences can be helpful, but God has given us the truth. Trust Scripture to be the authority and the Spirit to work in people's lives. You can't change anyone, but God can. Continually point people to the Word and to active steps of faith.

KEEP CONNECTING:

Think of ways to connect with group members during the week. Participation during your group meeting is always improved by time spent connecting with each other away from the group meeting. The more people are comfortable with and involved in each other's lives, the more they will look forward to being together. When people move beyond "being friendly" and "in the same group" to truly being friends who form a community, they come to group eager to engage, instead of merely attending.

Encourage group members with thoughts, commitments, or questions from the session by sending …

- › **emails.**
- › **texts.**
- › **or social networking messages.**

When possible, build community by planning or spontaneously inviting group members to join you outside of your regularly scheduled group time for …

- › **meals.**
- › **tasks.**
- › **or fun activities.**

❯ GROUP CONTACT INFORMATION

Name _____ Number _____
Email _____

Name _____ Number _____
Email _____

Name _____ Number _____
Email _____

Name _____ Number _____
Email _____

Name _____ Number _____
Email _____

Name _____ Number _____
Email _____

Name _____ Number _____
Email _____

Name _____ Number _____
Email _____

Name _____ Number _____
Email _____

Name _____ Number _____
Email _____

Name _____ Number _____
Email _____